USED FOR HIS GLORY

NORAH

USED FOR HIS GLORY On 46ST

NORAH

KS
Kravitz & Sons
INNOVATORS IN PUBLISHING, MARKETING AND ADVERTISING

Used for
His Glory On 46st

Kravitz and Sons LLC
204 E Arlington Blvd. Suite B
Greenville, NC 27858

Published by Kravitz and Sons LLC.

Spirituality and Psychology

ISBN: 979-8-89639-729-8 (sc)
ISBN: 979-8-89639-728-1 (e)

Table of Contents

Editorial Review

Used for His Glory On 46th Street is a heartfelt and inspiring journey of faith, transformation, and divine purpose. The author beautifully explores how ordinary people can become extraordinary instruments in God's plan when they surrender their lives to him. The narrative flows with sincerity, emotional dept, and spiritual insight, making it relatable for readers seeking hope, healing, and direction in their personal walk with faith.

This book's strongest element is its authenticity. The personal struggles, moments of doubt, and ultimate renewal are portrayed with honesty, allowing readers to connect deeply with the message. The pacing is engaging, and the themes of redemption, forgiveness, and spiritual growth are woven naturally throughout the story. This makes the book suitable for individual reflection as well as group study or devotional reading.

The Beginning

Before my life drastically changed, it had to begin somewhere. It began, at the stage of life when I was a baby and really didn't understand the circumstances that surrounded me. The first few years I was surrounded by my parents, sisters, and brothers. Before long, as my parents separated, all I noticed around me was two adults who were my grandparents and had made the choice to keep me. And it seemed as though my sisters and brothers had left me.

My grandparents gave me everything I needed at that point in my life. They supplied me with my own bedroom, but most nights I would climb out of my bed and go into their bedroom, where I would lay between them stretching my arms out touching them both. At that point in life, I did not realize it was teaching me to not be afraid to reach out. My grandpa would wake me up in the morning and allow me to see him make up the bed, teaching me the importance of keeping your home clean. My grandma would always allow me to hear her blessing the food and explain to me why we bless our food. Any time I got dirty, my grandma would take my clothes off, bathe me, and put me on some clean clothing, which taught me the importance of keeping myself clean.

They also drove me out to the country many times, where my grandpa's boss man owned farm and land. My grandpa would sometimes take me over to the horses, where he would pick me up and allow me to rub the horses, which allowed me to connect with the horses in a manner which brought peace to my mind. Being out there gave me a sense of feeling free and I didn't know that feeling would help me in the future. But sometimes I still find myself crying just noticing that my sisters and brothers weren't in my presence, and sometimes the tears was just my way of being grateful to just be alive and able to do more than just breath. Which was more than I could do during seizures.

After living with my grandparents for so long, one day, my eyes opened wide and I smiled as I spotted my mother coming towards me with her arms opened wide. She had traveled far to pick me up and take me home. I didn't know where home was or what it looked like. But I knew that wherever home was, my sisters and brothers would be there with me. When I found myself living with my family again, certain ones within the family were gone. My dad, one of my sisters, and one of my brothers were just not there. But over time I learned that my parents had separated, and my mother had enrolled us all into school where she wanted us to learn more, graduate and become a plus to society.

Over the course of twelve years, my mother went to night school, got into welding, and into upholstery, and all my mother's children went to school. Some chose to leave school early and go in different directions, some had chosen to finish school, graduate, and go in directions which help further their education or career. I was one who chose to finish school, and over the years it was a test for me to do well in school, since life presented me with illnesses which made it more challenging to remember and focus, including epilepsy and Chiari Malformation. But when I studied over a long period, done something repetitiously or hands-on, it helped make things easier to understand and remember. So, I stayed after school many times, done extra credit, and any day I couldn't make it to school due to being sick, one of my sisters would be kind enough to bring home my homework.

During my eleventh year of school, I went on a date with a schoolmate who really was nice but didn't interest me much. Our interests were very different, so we just ended up going separate ways. Then during my twelfth and last year of school, I dated again and found myself very interested in someone who I could talk to about anything, who loved getting out and traveling just as much as I did, and who I wanted to continue getting to know. When I graduated high school, my parents bought my graduation ring together, and my family attended the ceremony—a moment I'll always remember. And it left me with goals for my life. But my first and most important, was to get in better health where I would never go into another seizure, no longer be under so much medication, be open to more education, and become more independent.

After graduating, the gentleman I had been dating had already left the city, and sailed off on a Navy ship, and we had been keeping in touch through letters. During this time circumstances came up which changed the way I felt about myself and tested my strength in every way. One day, there I was sitting in a car waiting for someone to return. While waiting I found myself getting into a tight, getting out of the car, going up to the door and ringing the doorbell.

The person I rode with came to the door and then I quoted "May I use your restroom". They replied "Sure, I'm still looking for the material". And I walked into the house going straight to the restroom. After using the toilet and washing my hands, I reached for the doorknob. Then as I opened the door, quickly another hand pulled on my hand. And as I looked up, it was the very person I was riding with continuing to pull me. I began to scream no, we both began to pull in opposite directions, and from time to time I would reach for the nearest thing to grab on. By time we reached the master bedroom he had pulled me hard enough to yank me, picked me up, and then threw me on the bed.

My body hit the bed hard, as I landed on my back, and afterwards everything that took place led to more tears, saliva all over my body, my mouth covered any time I tried to scream, the words "shut the hell up, nobody can hear you", and an injection I didn't ask for. Following it all, he slowly rose saying "You could have made it easier, and if you say a word about it, no one will believe you". He then left the room, and I continued crying as I spread my hands out and saw blood on one where I had cut my hand. Then I noticed that he had gotten up, left the room, and I began to head for the door slowly due to the pain in my lower back. By time I reached the front door, he came from behind me and followed me out of the house, closing the door behind us. As we walked out, I could see the street, which was a familiar street. And I just wanted to get as far as I could from the area.

That evening, I was taking a bath, scrubbing myself hard and felt as if no matter how many times I scrubbed, the dirt remained. I cried seeing visions of his face, the hallway, and myself being thrown. Until I found myself reciting the twenty third psalm and began to lighten up on washing my body, rubbing it softly. Over the following months I did my best to stay away from anything that reminded me of that moment and that area.

Not long afterwards, the gentleman I had been dating had returned home, I was so happy to see him, and days later he had popped the question of "Will you marry me", with excitement I replied yes. He was still in the Navy, and we were married on Navy Base, then returned home where we had our wedding reception. Then, there we were married, and I knew we had a lot to learn, but were willing to learn together. During our first few years of marriage, my husband worked in the field he was trained for in the Navy, which was electronics. However, because he was a new employee, he was often the first to be let go during layoffs, which led us to move frequently including once living with my husband's mother.

I followed my husband every time we moved and listened to his words very closely, knowing I had never lived in my own home and were just learning about bills. Also knowing the seizures were still out of control, and how much I trusted my husband. Trusting him, I also shared with him a small portion of what I encountered at eighteen, just mentioned that I was raped, who done it, and where it was done, but couldn't go into details without crying or reliving it, because it was still fresh. My husband went into tears and stated, "He will never touch you again". I believed him and it rested my mind.

After moving one last time and settling into our own place, I was sleeping in bed one night and my husband slowly walked into our bedroom. He then woke me up, tapping on my shoulder and saying to me in a low voice, "Norah, I believe that we both would be better off apart". After waking up to those words, I just slowly sat up as tears began to fall from my eyes, and my husband didn't say another word. All I could say, in a soft voice, was "Why". He didn't reply, couldn't look me in the eye. So, I grabbed my pillow, walked out of the room going towards the living room, placed my pillow on the couch and cried even more crying myself to sleep.

Not long afterwards we did just what my husband suggested, moved out of the same home, but still talked. I began to get very depressed, found myself having seizures more often, and with everything I had already encountered, including the seizures, the incident on forty-six street, and slowly separating from the one I loved, I had to make a choice to either lose myself or fight for myself.

After living apart from my husband over the course of months, only seeing him on days when he came to visit me in my home, and crying during the nights we slept apart, we were going through a divorce. During the divorce, I sat quietly, following instructions, feeling numb and heartbroken. Later, that evening while sleeping alone, my tears began to slowly drop feeling heavier than ever and I found myself feeling down and remembering everything my husband and I both had done together. As time went on, I tried lifting my head every day and told myself, "I'm somebody".

Months later, I came across someone I had only seen once before. Someone who helped my mother take me to the hospital one evening while going into a seizure. They worked over the road and were working again when they spotted me and remembered my name calling it, saying, Mrs. Norah. I then turned around and remembered his face, but not his name.

He then reminded me of who he was and asked how I was doing. The conversation went on as we began to talk about both of our lives. I found out what he did as a driver, and he listened to me talking about how hard it was going through a divorce but not ready to give up on myself. He then asked me, "Would you like to learn about trucking"? My reply was, "I never thought about it, but I always loved traveling". Then I began to walk away saying, "I have to think about that". And he slipped a paper with his name and number on it into my hand as I continued walking away, hearing him say "It has been nice seeing you again".

As time went on, there I was thinking about all I had encountered and was still trying to get the seizures under control. Till one day, a friend named Jenifer said to me as we were taking a walk together, "You need a change in your life, something you can work with in a manner you like". And later that evening, while washing clothes, I found the number the gentlemen gave to me in my pants pocket by surprise and called him.

The next time the gentleman, Mr. Nathan Sanders, came through he allowed me to take a ride with him and see what his job was like. It was an experience for me which was very interesting. It gave me room to meet different people, see different places, work and be exposed to new things. By the time Mr. Nathan Sanders had left, we both had decided to give it a try, and months later in December, I was moving and starting a new journey.

We had my medical records transferred as I moved to a state called the Natural State. The seizures were still occurring, the nightmares would come up occasionally, but traveling and working over the course of eight years helped somehow.

Many times, I came across different people and situations which shed light and gave answers to questions I've always had about life in general. I listened to people from different states as they talked about the money market and different fields they worked in, they also shared with me the way of life where they lived, and some would share what they knew about the state of Florida, after finding out that's where I was from. Unloading the truck was a choice for truckers. And if you chose to unload, the pay was good. Sleeping in the sleeper, which resided in the truck, was very different from sleeping in your own bed at home. And required getting used to.

About a year later, I had chosen to move permanently to the Natural State, and Mr. Nathan Sanders had asked for my hand in marriage. Then over the course of nine years so much took place as Nathan and I lived together as husband and wife. We continued working over the road trucking for miles, had two of Nathan's sons living with us during our first year, we drove the Cadillac to Church every Sunday we were home, I had a miscarriage during our second year which required me to be on bedrest for a while, weeks later went back on the road, and I also continued seeking help to get the seizures under control, from a Neurologist well known in the state of Arkansas, Doctor Anthony Baker.

By time Doctor Baker had tried different medications for the seizures, his last suggestion was a new procedure that had worked for many patients but required more tests to be done prior to the procedure. Around this time Nathan and I also had a disagreement. Nathan was straight forward when it came to what he wanted, and by surprise one day he said, "I would like to have an open marriage. Not knowing if he was joking, I just replied with, "But I wouldn't". I only wanted to be with my husband in that manner and wanted to be the only woman with him. That opened my eyes to how different Nathan, and I viewed marriage and made me watch him closer.

Soon after, time was getting closer for surgery. Nathan said he couldn't get enough time off work for my surgery and suggested that I try staying with family during the procedure, with his words to bring me back home after healing and recovering. Being obedient, I moved back to my home state temporally for surgery, my medical records were transferred, and the doctors took me through more tests before proceeding with surgery. Nathan visited frequently and stayed with me whenever he came into town.

Then by surprise I received a box filled with pictures and other items that belonged to Nathan and me, which were broken and sent to me by someone unknown. Not only unknown but also residing at the very address where Nathan and I resided married. I then called Nathan to see what was going on, and before long, I had to put all the tests on hold and return to the natural state where I found myself going through divorce procedures again, but for a change I had the knowledge of what and why I was going through. And my tears were not tears of sorrow, but tears of understanding and letting go. This man who was once connected to me in such a manner, I was disconnecting from in such a manner that allowed me to heal.

After nine years of marriage and one year of engagement, we were unable to reach an agreement regarding our perspectives on the fundamental nature of marriage. But afterwards I returned to my home state, went through the surgery for seizures which required months to heal, and started a journey which led to better health.

Words of Wisdom

As a person and individual, I have been blessed to experience things in different fields and among different places. And the greatest thing I found among it all was a purpose for every living thing.

Even we, as people, have a purpose. Which was instilled in us from the beginning. And that purpose will remain with us until the end. But until we walk in it, we will fall into anything else which tempts us.

And if we feel as though it's hard to know or find our purpose, then it's important that we ask and be patient knowing the answer will come to us. Life presents answers before us every day. We just must be ready and willing to receive the answers. And not everyone will receive the same answers, because we all are unique.

Your purpose awaits you, and only you can walk in it.

Chapter 1

Learning to Trust His Plan

Familiar Grounds

At this point in my life, I had been given the opportunity to start fresh. I had gone through surgery to help improve the seizures, which required doctors to remove a small part of the left temporal lobe, and had chosen not to remain married to someone who did not desire the same as I did in a marriage. And after surgery, during my first doctor's visit, my doctor had let me know that I had only regained ten percent of my memories. He then wanted to do more tests to see what the best decisions would be concerning the next step.

After finishing the tests, my doctor, Doctor Fernendez, had decided the best avenue would be to try rehab, and he set me up an appointment with Florida Rehab Services. After getting into Florida Rehab Services, they did more tests and suggested that my best bet would be starting over in school at third grade level. Shortly afterwards, I was enrolled into an Adult High School, where they tested me for the second time, and agreed with Rehab Services to start me off on third grade level. Over the course of ten months, tending Blake Adult High School, I sat there listening to great teachers, studying day and night, and relearning third grade work to twelfth. And afterwards I had to go see Doctor Fernendez before going any further with education. With Doctor Fernendez approval, months later there I was enrolling into college taking up massage therapy.

While in college, certain symptoms started occurring which required me to visit my doctor again. And as doctor Fernendez searched for answers to the symptoms, he couldn't pinpoint the problem and suggested bedrest for weeks. While resting the symptoms didn't improve, and someone who knew where the surgery was first recommended, Mrs. Johnson, suggested returning to UAMS, which meant heading back to the natural state. I had to think about this decision, would my health allow me to move again, how long it would take to transfer my medical records, where would I stay until I find my own place, and most importantly, would it help find the answer to what was causing the issues in my health? Including a pain that was shooting down from the back of my scull to my spine.

Not long afterwards, I decided to take a chance on returning to the natural state, with hope of finding relief. After returning, I was first instructed to get plenty of rest. Months later, my medical records had been transferred back to the natural state, and I had been reinstated into rehab services.

This time around, after attending college in Florida, Arkansas Rehab Services suggested giving college another try. And my new doctor, Doctor Stanson, kept a close eye on everything. Till she found the cause of the pain and suggested finding a doctor who specialized in Chiari Malformation. Doctor Stanson also suggested seeing a psychiatrist. In her words, "Sometimes our pain is not only due to illnesses, but also stress or something internal".

Over the next few months, I listened to my doctor and case worker, by setting up an appointment with a psychiatrist, and helped launch a small ministry. The ministry was headed by an individual acquainted with my former spouse, Nathan. They led the ministry in a new direction, and I remained in the ministry long enough to witness it start growing and left not long before time came around to see my psychiatrist.

The day came, and I caught the city bus to my appointment. After arriving, I had to sit in the waiting room. Until my name was called and someone walked me to the office where my psychiatrist was sitting. Upon entering the room, I observed the psychiatrist sitting in her chair, facing me. Extending her hand, she introduced herself by saying, "I am Doctor Himes, and it is a pleasure to meet you, Mrs. Norah, did I say the name right"? I then replied by saying "Yes, Ma'am, some don't". And we both laughed, which made the atmosphere a little easier. Then as we began to talk, Doctor Himes just wanted me to tell her a little about my life. I began by mentioning what it was like to have many siblings and how I missed them when we were apart. And I ended my talk with goals I had while in high school and what it was like getting married at a very young age.

After talking for a while and getting silent after mentioning being married very young, Doctor Himes asked, "Have you ever tried hypnosis"? My reply was "No, what is hypnosis"? She explained, "Hypnosis is when someone is put to sleep to relax the mind and answer questions without mental barriers. Sometimes we suppress memories to avoid feeling pain from certain moments in our lives". I replied with, "If it can help the situation, sure". Doctor Himes then recommended that I lie down on the couch, after which she started the hypnosis. By time it was over, Doctor Himes suggested support group without telling me what type. All she did was hand me a note that listed the date, time, and address.

Being obedient, I went to the meeting days later and was welcomed the moment I arrived. I then sat and listened to the stories of many people. I found myself crying during some stories, and the two things which everyone had in common were feeling violated and alone. After a while, I heard a story very close to what I experienced and just froze. I could see myself reaching for the doorknob, being pulled and grabbing everything I could, screaming but not being heard, being picked up and slammed on my back as if I was in a wrestling match, feeling something wet on my body, having my mouth covered, and hearing the words "No one would believe you". And when they finished their story, I asked "May I go"?

I then stood up and introduced myself saying, "My name is Norah, and I am a survivor of rape. In my case, it wasn't a stranger". As I shared my story, many were moved to tears, and after, the group rose from their seats, clapped as I wiped away the tears, and slowly gathered for a hug. Until that day, I had never truly revisited that moment at eighteen or allowed myself to cry openly without concern for being seen. I could feel my body shaking at one moment and my mind rejoicing towards the end realizing I wasn't alone in my situation, I wasn't strange or different, but I was strong enough to say no when it happened and say no to giving control of my life to that one moment.

Upon returning home that day, I offered a prayer, affirming faith in God as my healer and redeemer, and entrusted my concerns in the name of Jesus.

Although I had left one ministry, inside of me still lied the desire to find a ministry in which I could continue growing in. Since I had plans to go back to college, I avoided roles that demanded a lot of time or effort as I visited different ministries.

I also got out using public transportation, learning the city, I had not yet decided whether to make it home or not. While learning I came across places which made history, which included the Clinton Library, the State Capital, and the old and new Veterans Cemetery. By surprise I also came across information on my dad after hearing from certain family members. After all the years I had lived in the Natural State. I never knew that my dad, whom I haven't lived or chatted with much since around the age of three. He was born, given birth to, in this state where I have trucked, lived, and received treatments from doctors. I always wanted to sit down with him, ask questions concerning him including where he was from, what qualities to look for in a man, and simply did he love me and the rest of his children.

The answer to many of my questions concerning him was on the grounds I walked on, in the state where I resided, and in the hearts of a few who known my dad but wouldn't say a word about him. This news made me realize it wasn't a mistake where I resided. In a way, it was home, where my dad was given life and brought into existence. And it made me realize how life brings answers right before you.

I figured, if it was meant for me to find out more about my dad, then it would come to me naturally here where I reside. And I started focusing on finding a church home and deciding if Arkansas is where I'm planning on attending college.

Chapter 2

Love In the Mix of It All

Meeting Him

While learning about the city and waiting for the answer concerning whether Arkansas will be the place where I continue college, I looked up information on the colleges in the city where I resided. I also came across people who worked in hospitals, ministries, police stations, and other places. Which included a neighbor of mine who shared with me a few safe ways to meet people. Including certain websites.

One website she mentioned I didn't receive many remarks, nor left many. Until one day when I received a chirp. The individual who left the chirp chatted very respectfully, and later our chats became regular and clean. I liked that, till a couple months later, I found my membership expiring and gave the person my phone number hoping to continue chatting by phone. He enjoyed the conversations himself, and we continued chatting by phone over the course of another month.

Till one day, this gentleman by the name of Johnathon Williams asked me out on a date. His way of asking was by mentioning different restaurants in the city and asking what type of restaurant I liked. I knew what he was up to and felt comfortable enough to tell him what type, which was Chinese buffet with seafood, and we ended up trying the place he suggested.

The restaurant was located near a college, and after Johnathon opened the door for me to the restaurant, a waitress then seated us. Once seated comfortably in a booth, we began our conversation, received our beverages, and I proceeded to approach the buffet first. We then returned to the booth and began to chat again. It was easy to chat with Johnathon; we chatted about everything from our past relationships to our likes and dislikes. By the time everything was finished, we had eaten dinner, tipped the waitress, paid our bills, and Johnathon drove me home. There, we hugged and said our goodbyes. It was a while before we saw each other again, and I really enjoyed our first date.

While still waiting for the date on which I will start college, Johnathon and I continued dating. Majority of the time, it wasn't in the city where we spent time. Instead, it was up in the mountains. Which included Mount Magazine known as the highest mountain in Arkansas, Petit Jean Mountain, and Mount Nebo. We just took our time going up the mountains and getting to know each other.

The day arrived when my rehabilitation case worker contacted me to provide the details regarding the college I would be attending. My grade point average on the test I completed did not meet the requirements for my preferred college. But it was high enough to get into a college very well known in the Little Rock area. Prior to starting college, I had the privilege of being given a tour of the campus two days after receiving the call. While walking the campus, it just amazed me to see myself standing on such grounds with the bill paid in full. All the students we passed, the teachers I met, and each part of the campus with its own character. I was saying to myself, "This is an opportunity I will not waste".

Due to the date being too close to the last semester in college, I had to wait until the beginning of the following year to attend. While waiting on the day on which my college classes would start, one moment arose which I wasn't expecting at that time. Johnathon and I went out to see a movie one day, at a theater which resided inside of a mall. After watching the movie, we walked around the mall until we came up to a jewelry store. Johnathon said he wanted to check out the men's watches, and we walked into the store checking them out. Johnathon then pulled the salesperson aside and requested something else.

Not knowing what he requested, I saw the salesperson coming from the back of the store with something else besides a watch. And when they put the jewelry on the countertop, Johnathon picked it up, and it was a diamond wedding band. He then said to me, "Norah, will you marry me"? My right hand then went over my mouth, and with excitement I said, "Yes I will, but let me add to this". I then showed the salesperson another ring, a man's wedding band in which I wanted Johnathon to have and said, "Yes Johnathon, yes", as we embraced each other.

Two Becoming One in Matrimony

After buying the rings, days later, Johnathon and I shared the news with both of our families, inviting them all. Everyone on both sides was saying the date we chose was a good time for them. Until something came up where we had to change the date to a few months earlier than we originally planned. That cut the number of attendants in half.

The wedding day came around, all went well, and we went on our honeymoon in the city of Hot Springs. The place where we stayed was right off the river with a jacuzzi tub, king size bed, large living area, and outdoor patio area. It was very romantic and we didn't want to leave. But three days later, we did and I made sure we had pictures of the place before leaving.

As time went on Johnathon and I woke up every morning to one another. During the week Johnathon would get ready for work early in the morning, and I would cook breakfast making sure he ate before heading out. After Johnathon left, I would get a few more zees before getting up and cleaning around the house.

Johnathon had a daughter named Crystal and a son we called Junior, because he was named after his dad. Crystal was in her twenties and in between homes. While searching for a new home, we welcomed her in, and she searched for not only a new home but also a different job. She had many interests and talents but had to make the decision of which one she wanted to shoot for. Junior was in college and had already got involved with one he was very close to. She touched his heart, they both had dreams, and wanted to reach for their dreams, with hope of doing it together.

As time went on, Crystal and Junior continued shooting for their goals, and in the process, everything didn't go as expected, but it all went in a direction which led them to having their own children, getting into their own homes, and finding jobs where they could use their talents.

A year after getting married, Johnathon and I were living alone and Johnathon was still waking up early, getting ready for work five days a week. We started getting out more, going to visit family, taking walks in the parks and along the rivers, going fishing, and making sure each of us kept up with our doctor's appointments. And we decided to search some day for another church home.

Chapter 3

(Walking in Her Purpose)

Moving Ahead

At this point in marriage and in life, I started searching for a support group related to the illness I was diagnosed with. No in-person options were available, but several online ones were found. And while chatting online, I came across others who also desired in-person options, and we started meeting together supporting one another. Before long, our gatherings turned into meetings, and we began to create the first CM in-person support group in the capital of Arkansas.

As planned, Johnathon and I also started looking for a new church home. Until one day we settled into one we visited more than once. The name of the ministry was New Hope Ministry, which wasn't far from our home. And not long after we became members, the pastor, Pastor Newton, noticed the work I was putting into creating a support group and offered to allow me the use of the church building for our meetings. I was grateful, as I accepted the offer and began to put together a meeting every four months to spread awareness and give support to those near the Little Rock area fighting Chiari Malformation.

As Pastor Newton stood back and joined us for the meetings, she liked what she saw and offered to train me as an Administrator Pastor. I asked what all is required, and she replied, "Just what you are doing here, but also tending our training sessions". I then answered by saying, "I'm taking up college classes soon, so I won't be able to do anything which requires too much time. Pastor Newton then replied saying, "I understand and we can work you in part time".

Over a long period, once a month Pastor Newton would work me in, where I spoke before the ministry teaching on Biblical Topics. I would pray and study on topics the Lord laid on my heart, over the course of a week prior to the date, make sure my uniform was drycleaned, arrive early the day I was scheduled to teach, and spend a little time praying before speaking.

Three times a year, around January, June, and December we put together a Chiari Support Group. Which always started with a hearty welcome. We also had information printed on Chiari Malformation, which was always laid out on a table where everyone could view and take a copy for themselves. A professional speaker was always present, trained as a speaker myself, I would cover for any speaker who couldn't make it for some reason. We also had food and prizes, and most importantly we supported every individual in the room. Which included those who joined us just to see what we were all about.

Weeks later, it was time to begin my studies at Pulaski Tech, one of the leading technical schools in the area. This turn around, it wasn't Massage Therapy I signed up for, instead, it was Business Administration. I wanted to learn more about business and have the support group registered as a nonprofit organization. I also wanted to work towards getting my driver license. This meant ongoing doctor visits for seizure treatment, with the potential for a reduced medication dose.

While going to Pulaski Tech, it was an experience to chat with the teachers and get so much information from them. Working beside the other students gave me a since of belonging and an urge to keep learning. Seeing every part of the college, let me know how far I had come. Until the end of the first semester, when I received a call from my doctor's office.

My primary doctor had finally gotten an appointment for me with the only doctor in the state of Arkansas who specialized in surgery for Chiari Malformation, Doctor Anthony Mason. She informed me that I would need to postpone college, since my appointment was coming up soon and the procedures would take a while. The following day, when I arrived at Pulaski Tech, I headed straight to the front office and inquired, "Who should I talk to about putting my classes on hold for a medical reason?" The lady I spoke to, Mrs. Anderson, then said to me, "You need to speak to Mr. Thompson, and he'll be with you in a minute".

Mr. Thompson came out of his office shortly afterwards and introduced himself to me along with inviting me into his office. We then sat in his office as I explained to him my situation. And by time our conversation was over, he was wishing me the best concerning the surgery. I then walked out of Pulaski Tech, not knowing if I would ever return, but happy to experience my first semester where so much knowledge is in the palm of your hand.

One week later, I arrived at the office of Dr. Anthony Mason. And when I finally saw his face, he was walking into the room where I had been sitting and waiting patiently to see him. He introduced himself, reviewed my medical records, and explained what the surgery would involve if I agreed to proceed. Once I heard him out, my only question was how soon it could be scheduled. Doctor Mason then told me, in another four weeks, and I responded, "Let's proceed." We both then stood up and shook hands, as he quoted "Nice meeting you Mrs. Norah

Williams". And his nurse came in with papers to sign and instructions as he was leaving out.

Johnathon had to take time off his job to be there with me through surgery. So, he submitted his notice at work, and it was approved. I also had to request time off with the ministry we were in, and temporarily cancel all the Chiari Support meetings, until months after surgery. Two weeks before surgery, I had to drink a cleansing liquid and shave the back half of my head. It was an experience seeing myself with very short hair only from the front of my head.

When the day of my surgery finally came, Johnathon was right by my side. He held my hand until he had to go, just as the doctor entered the room. Doctor Mason then talked with me a little, as Nurse Thomas came in. She then gave me a shot which soon put me to sleep, and the surgery began. The surgery was over four hours later, but I was still asleep. Till I woke up during the night and found Johnathon beside me. He was sleeping in a Lazy Boy recliner which was set next to the bed. The following day, my nurse had another bed placed beside mine, in case Johnathon slept overnight again. Johnathon then saw the bed as we both laughed, and every night that's where he slept.

I stayed five nights on a liquid diet while Johnathon ate well. Doctor Mason came in to see me for the last two days, making sure everything went well and looking into my eyes. Asking me, can I see him, making sure I can open my eyes. He also asked other questions, till he said you are well enough to go home. For now, you should remain on bedrest and not do things by yourself.

That evening, Johnathon and I were lying in our own bed. It felt so good to be home resting my head. Over the following month I couldn't do anything alone. Eating, bathing, and even walking required a helping hand. Johnathon was there, and Junior came to visit sometimes. They assisted me until I became better at walking and could do things alone.

Eight weeks later, there I was up and moving again. However, changes needed to be made to continue healing, and they were. Including the decision to retire from the position which was given to me in the ministry, and the choice to return to college, I decided not to. But one thing we kept a hold to for just a little longer was the support group. Till seven years had passed and it was time to close.

During my next visit to see Doctor Mason, he sat there prescribing only one prescription, and it wasn't for seizures. By time I noticed, he was gone and that's all he had for me. I had been taken off every medication they ever prescribed for seizures. And I didn't know how to take the news, except one day at a time.

Over the following month, I found myself still reaching for my nightstand, forgetting that I was no longer taking medicine, feeling nothing beneath my hands. As time went on, it was very different to not feel drowsy or drained. And I learned to replace medicine with vitamins and foods which help the brain. My head began to feel lighter; my eyes were easier to open. I could hear without a ringing sound in my ear, and my body just seemed energized.

I no longer found myself waking up in the middle of my sleep, and everything which I had experienced between both surgeries had set a pattern for my life. From restoring the memories of my past to reeducating my mind, learning a deep and personal side of myself, and growing in an atmosphere where life was just new and different.

Others played a role in my daily life, including my husband, our immediate family and family from both sides. Also, coworkers, and friends who had been there through it all. Some people had come in and out of my life since high school and didn't understand the difference they had begun to see in me. Because to understand, they had to be there every step of the way, including when things got tough.

News Which Leads Back to 46TH Street

Around this time, and while closing the on-line Chiari Support Group, someone who had not spoken to me in so long replied to a hello to which our grandson James had left on my Facebook page. It was someone who knew a little pertaining to what I had encountered at eighteen. They replied to the hello with hello, a few words, and news. The news of someone being very sick and maybe on their death bed.

Due to the fact, the one who was sick was the very one whom I had an encounter with at eighteen, the only thing that came out of my mouth was, "My prayers are with the family". God had relieved me from the trauma that haunted me at the age of eighteen. And gave me the heart to forgive and speak kind words.

That individual chatted a little longer and then said goodbye. Afterwards, I said to myself "It's time to go down forty-six street again". Not knowing what type of reaction, it would bring out of me. Nor if I will remember what took place in full details. Just knowing, it's no longer that eighteen-year-old who would be traveling down the same street.

Instead, it's the one who has fought to come out of many seizures and nightmares of 46th Street, who gained enough courage to rise after divorce and traveled from state to state learning what trucking is all about, who has had the honor of studying in college and teaching in ministry, and who has said no with tears in her eyes, she's now ready and willing to return to forty-sixth street.

www.ingramcontent.com/pod-product-compliance
Ingram Content Group UK Ltd.
Pitfield, Milton Keynes, MK11 3LW, UK
UKHW062257290726
14090UKWH00017B/752